GREEN DAY BULLET IN A BIBLE

Special thanks to Rob Cavallo, Pat Magnerella and Tyler Willingham

Transcribed by Danny Begelman

Contents

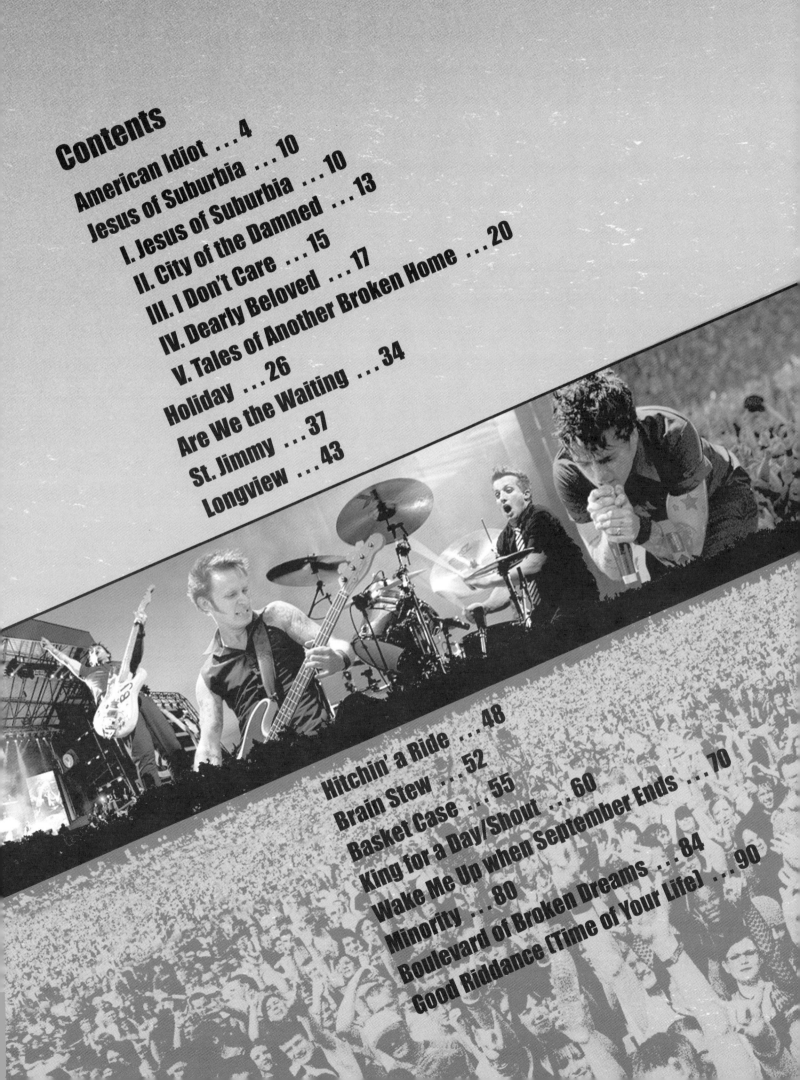

AMERICAN IDIOT

Words by BILLIE JOE
Music by GREEN DAY

American Idiot - 6 - 4
25748

8

Interlude:
w/ad lib. vocal

w/Rhy. Fig. 1 *(Elec. Gtr. 1)*

Repeat as needed | Last time

Verse 3:

w/Rhy. Fig. 1 *(Elec. Gtr. 1)*

Don't want to be an A-mer-i-can id-i-ot, one na-tion con-trolled_

w/Rhy. Fig. 1 *(Elec. Gtr. 1) 1st 2 meas. only*

_ by the me-di-a. In-for-ma-tion age_ of hys-ter-i-a

Chorus:

N.C.

Elec. Gtr. 2 resume chorus fig. simile

is call-ing out to id-i-ot A-mer-i-ca. Wel-come to a new_

_ kind of ten-sion all a-cross the a-li-en-a-tion,_

Outro:

JESUS OF SUBURBIA

Moderately ♩ = 144

I. Jesus of Suburbia

Verse:

Words by BILLIE JOE
Music by GREEN DAY

1. I'm the son of rage and love,___ the
2. Get my tel - e - vi - sion fix,___

Je - sus of Sub - ur - bi - a, from the bi - ble of___ "none of the a - bove,"___ on a
sit - ting on my cru - ci - fix. The liv - ing room___ in my pri - vate womb,___ while the

stead - y di - et of___
moms and Brads are a - way.___

12

Jesus of Suburbia - 16 - 3
25748

II. City of the Damned

14

III. I Don't Care

16

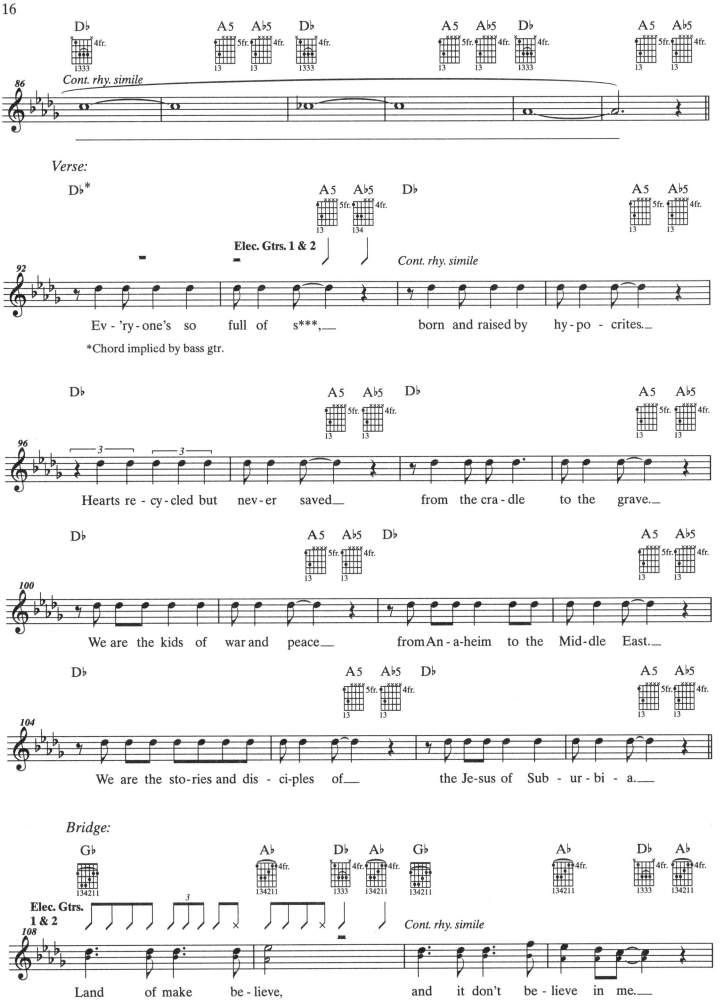

Verse:

*Chord implied by bass gtr.

Ev - 'ry-one's so full of s***,___ born and raised by hy-po - crites.___

Hearts re - cy-cled but nev-er saved___ from the cra-dle to the grave.___

We are the kids of war and peace___ from An-a-heim to the Mid-dle East.___

We are the sto-ries and dis - ci-ples of___ the Je-sus of Sub - ur-bi - a.___

Bridge:

Land of make be - lieve, and it don't be - lieve in me.___

18

20

Moderately slow ♩ = 72

V. Tales of Another Broken Home

Interlude:

1. To

Elec. Gtrs. 1 & 2

Verse:

w/Rhy. Fig. 3 *(Elec. Gtrs. 1 & 2)* 7 times

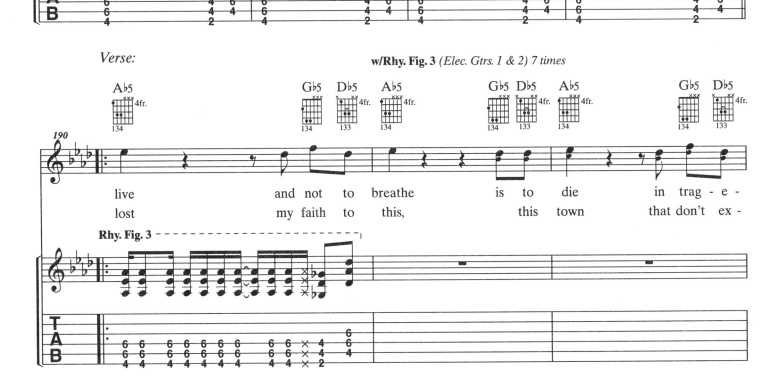

live

and not to breathe

is to die

in trag-e-

lost

my faith to this,

this town

that don't ex-

Rhy. Fig. 3

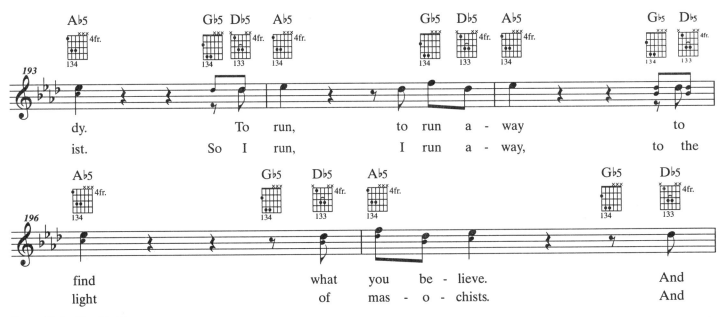

dy.

To run,

to run a - way

to

ist.

So I run,

I run a - way,

to the

find

what you be - lieve.

And

light

of mas - o - chists.

And

22

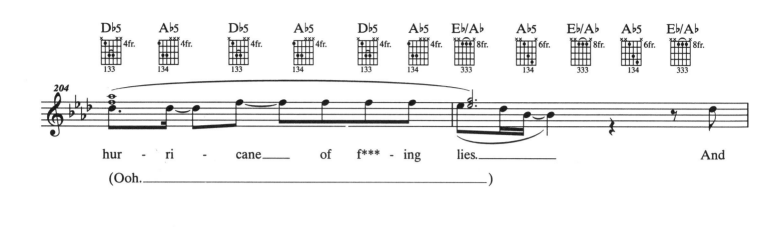

hur - ri - cane_____ of f***-ing lies._____ And
(Ooh._____)

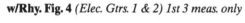

w/Rhy. Fig. 4 *(Elec. Gtrs. 1 & 2) 1st 3 meas. only*

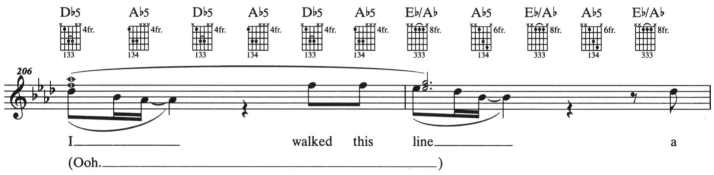

I_____ walked this line_____ a
(Ooh._____)

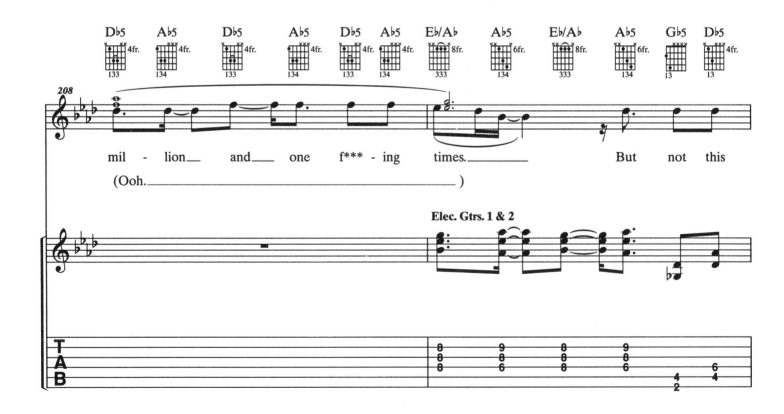

mil - lion____ and____ one f***-ing times._____ But not this
(Ooh._____)

Elec. Gtrs. 1 & 2

Outro:

w/Rhy. Fig. 3 *(Elec. Gtrs. 1 & 2) 4 times*

HOLIDAY

Words by BILLIE JOE
Music by GREEN DAY

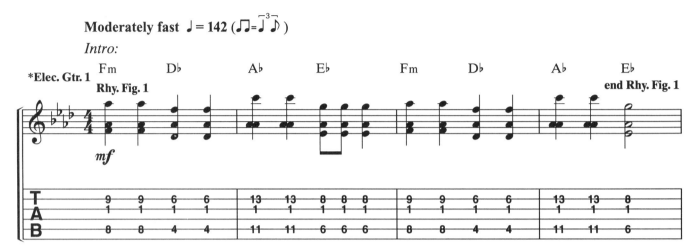

*Elec. Gtr. 1 is capoed at 1st fret but written in actual pitch. Tablature indicating 1st fret is played open with capo.

Elec. Gtr. 1 cont. in slashes

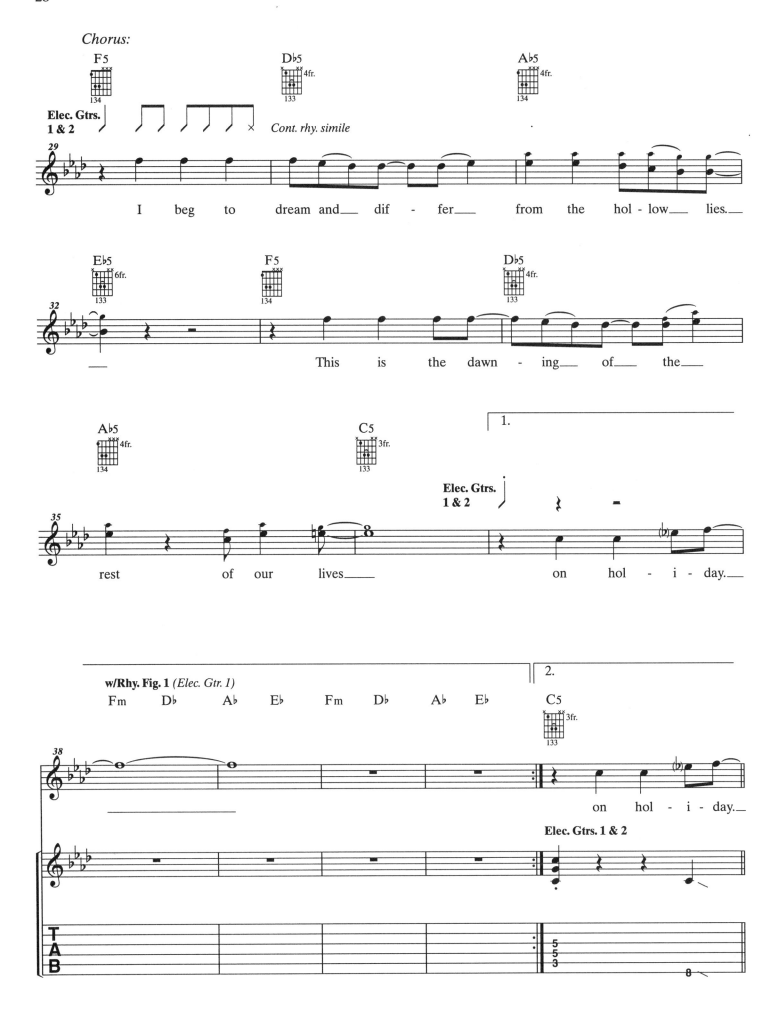

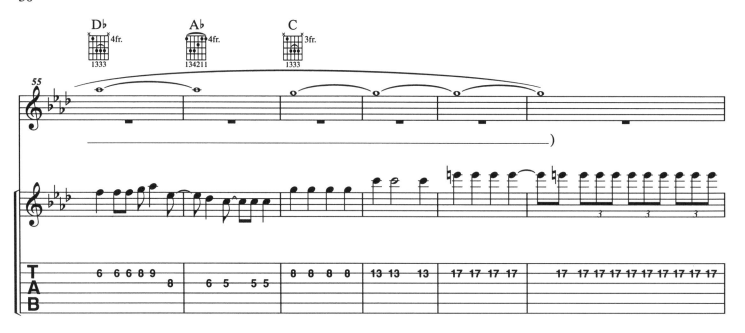

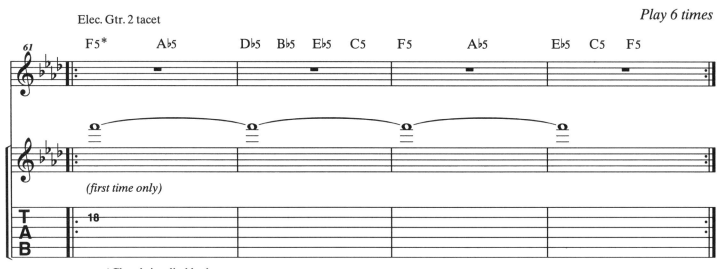

*Chords implied by bass gtr.

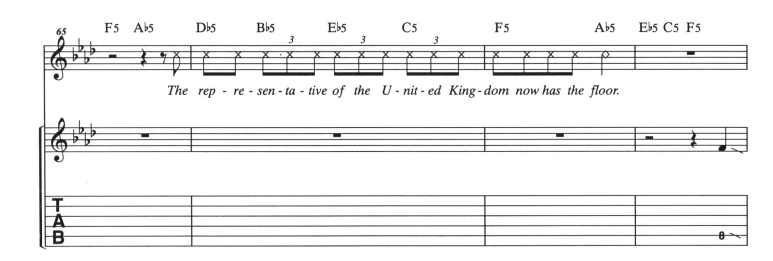

The rep - re - sen - ta - tive of the U - nit - ed King - dom now has the floor.

Bridge:

Elec. Gtrs. 1 & 2 tacet

Zieg Heil to the Pres-i-dent gas-man, bombs a-way is your pun-ish-ment. Pul-ver-ize the

Eif - fel Tow-ers, who crit-i-cize your gov-ern-ment. Bang, bang goes the bro-ken glass and

kill all the fags that don't a-gree. Tri-als by fire___ set-ting fires___ is not a way that's

meant for me. Just 'cause...
(Hey, hey, hey, hey,

32

ARE WE THE WAITING

Words by BILLIE JOE
Music by GREEN DAY

36

Are We the Waiting - 3 - 3
25748

ST. JIMMY

Words by BILLIE JOE
Music by GREEN DAY

Moderately fast ♩ = 136

Intro:

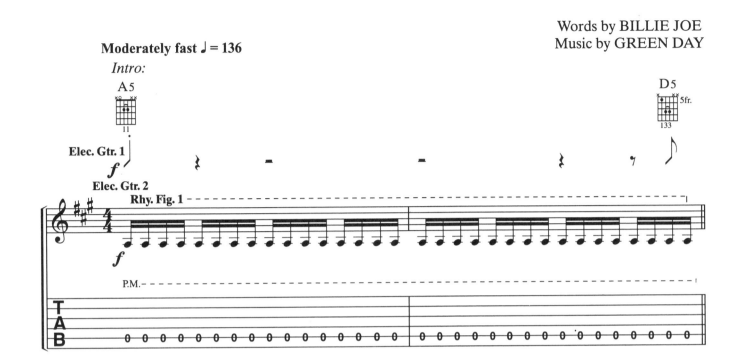

Verse 1:

w/Rhy. Fig. 1 *(Elec. Gtr. 2) 3 times*

Saint Jim-my's com-ing down___ a-cross the al-ley-way.___ Up on the bou-le-vard___ like a

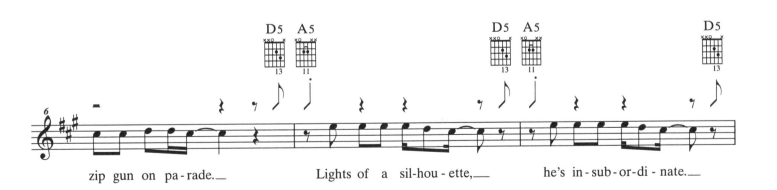

zip gun on pa-rade.___ Lights of a sil-hou-ette,___ he's in-sub-or-di-nate.___

38

St. Jimmy - 6 - 2
25748

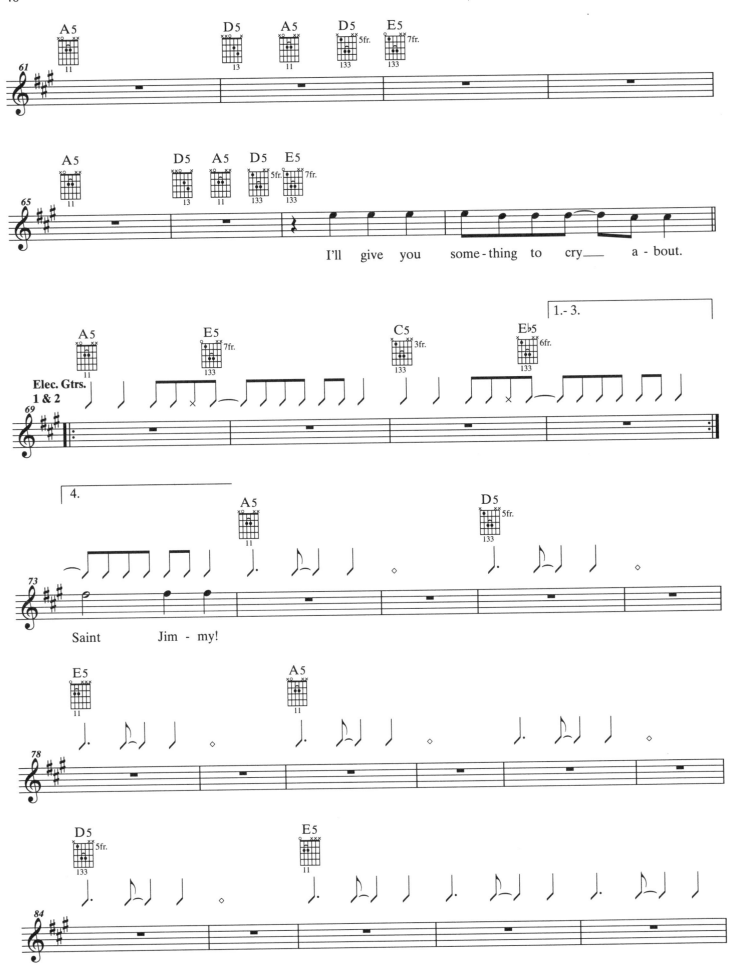

I'll give you some-thing to cry___ a-bout.

Saint Jim - my!

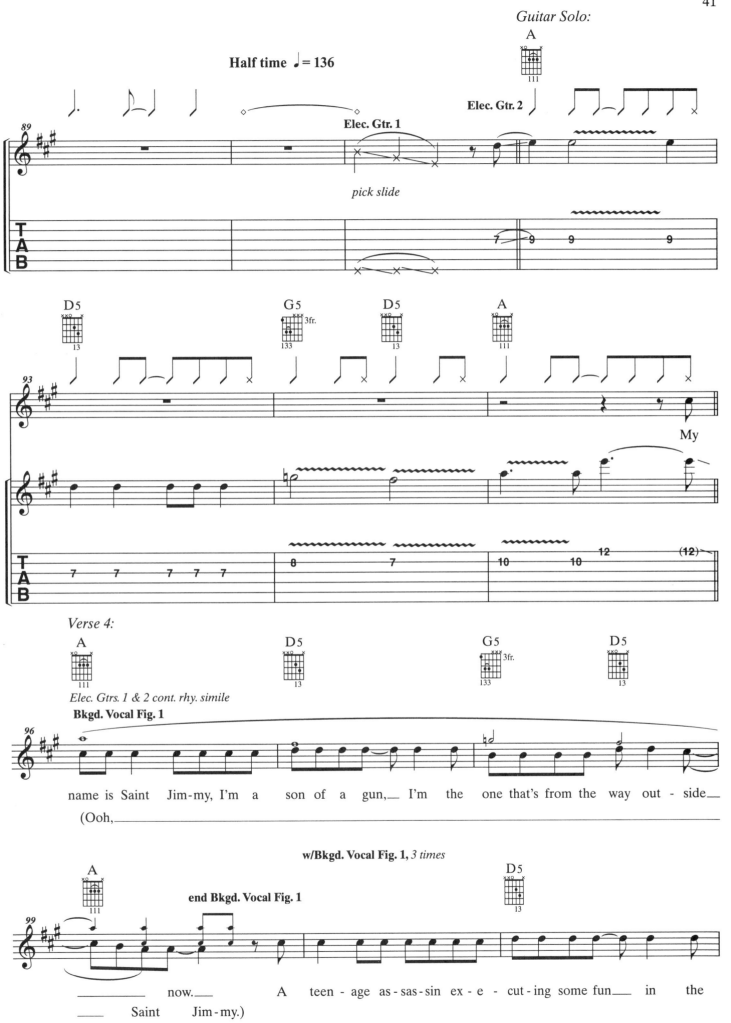

42

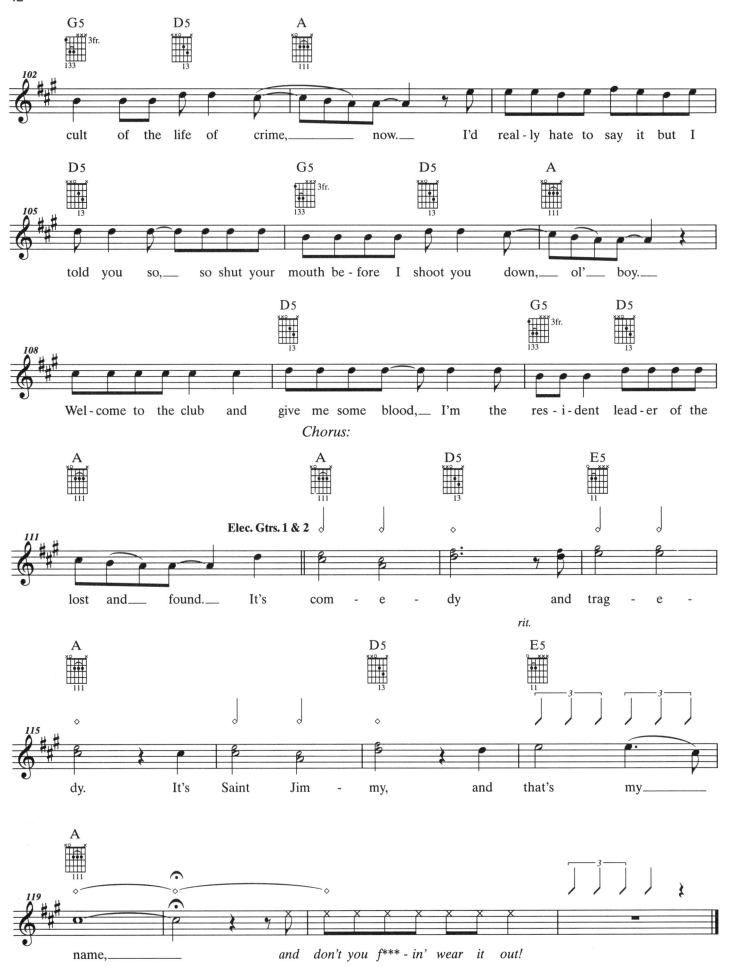

LONGVIEW

Lyrics by BILLIE JOE
Music by GREEN DAY

*Tune down 1/2 step:
⑥ = E♭ ③ = G♭
⑤ = A♭ ② = B♭
④ = D♭ ① = E♭

Moderately ♩ = 140

*Recording sounds a half step lower than written.

**Chords implied by bass gtr.

Verses 1 & 2:

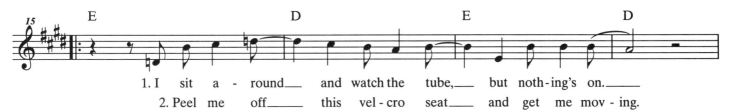

1. I sit a - round__ and watch the tube,__ but noth-ing's on.__
2. Peel me off__ this vel - cro seat__ and get me mov - ing.

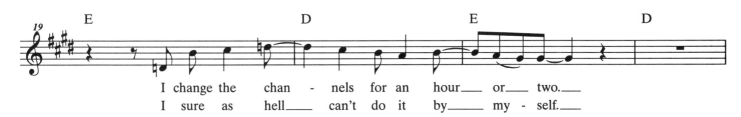

I change the chan - nels for an hour__ or__ two.__
I sure as hell__ can't do it by__ my - self.__

Twid - dle my thumbs just for a bit.__ I'm sick of all__ the same old s***;__
I'm feel - ing like a dog in heat,__ barred in - doors from__ the sum - mer street.__

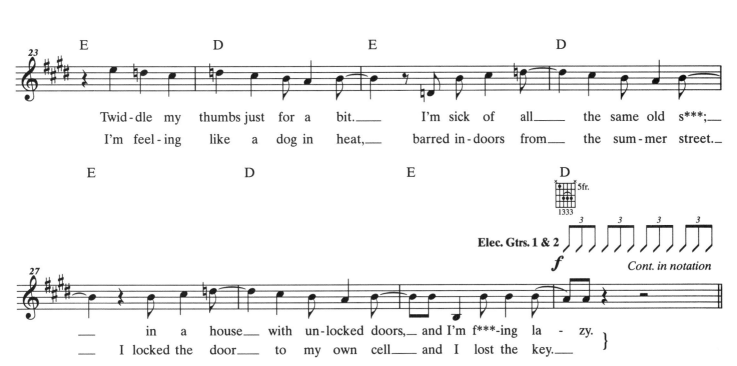

__ in a house__ with un - locked doors,__ and I'm f***-ing la - zy.
__ I locked the door__ to my own cell__ and I lost the key.__

Chorus:

*Chords implied by bass gtr.

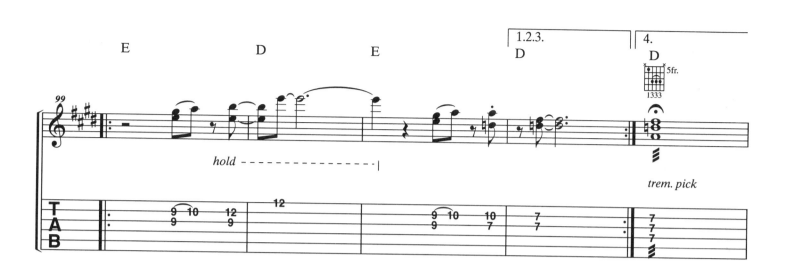

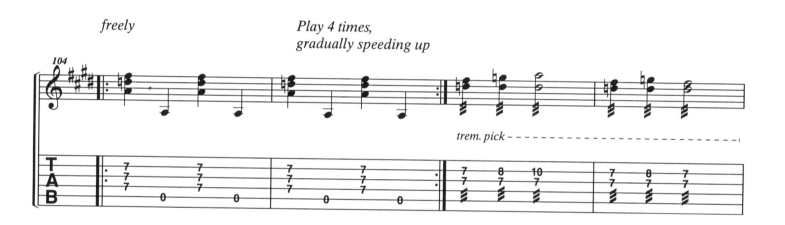

HITCHIN' A RIDE

Hitchin' a Ride - 4 - 2
25748

50

51

Hitchin' a Ride - 4 - 4
25748

BRAIN STEW

*Tune down 1/2 step:

⑥ = E♭ ③ = G♭

⑤ = A♭ ② = B♭

④ = D♭ ① = E♭

Lyrics by BILLIE JOE
Music by GREEN DAY

Moderately slow ♩ = 76

Intro:

A5   G5   F#5   F5   E5   A5   G5   F#5   F5   E5

Elec. Gtrs. 1 & 2

Cont. rhy. simile

Recording sounds a half step lower than written.

Verse 1:

A5   G5   F#5   F5   E5

I'm hav-ing trou-ble try-ing to sleep.

A5   G5   F#5   F5   E5

I'm count-ing sheep but run-ning out.

A5   G5   F#5   F5   E5

As time ticks by, and still I try.

A5   G5   F#5   F5   E5

No rest for cross-tops in my mind. (crowd) On my own. Here we go.

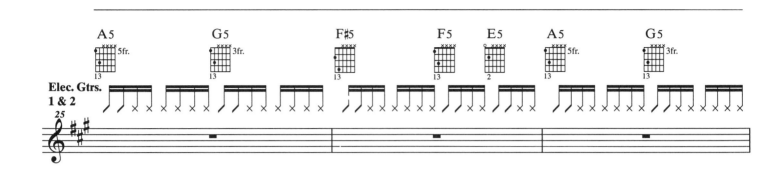

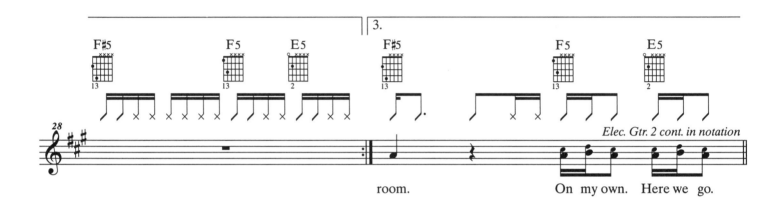

room.

On my own. Here we go.

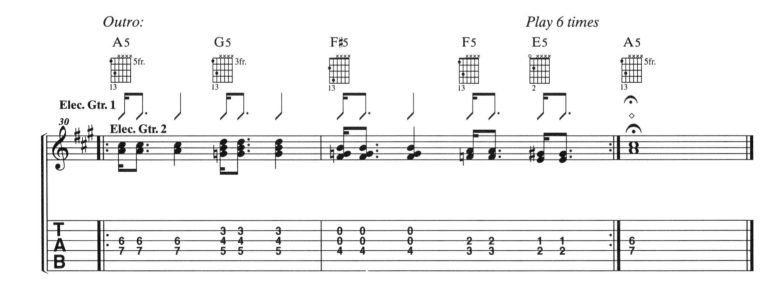

BASKET CASE

58

Outro:

KING FOR A DAY/SHOUT

62

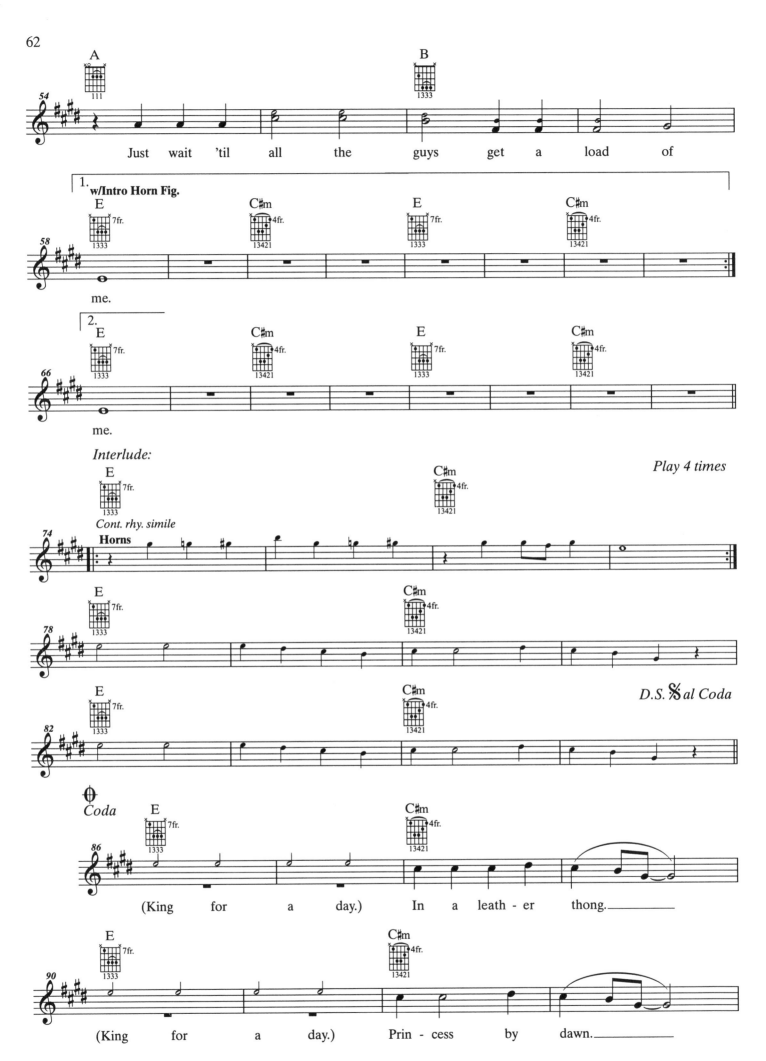

Words and Music by
O'KELLY ISLEY, RONALD ISLEY
and RUDOLPH ISLEY

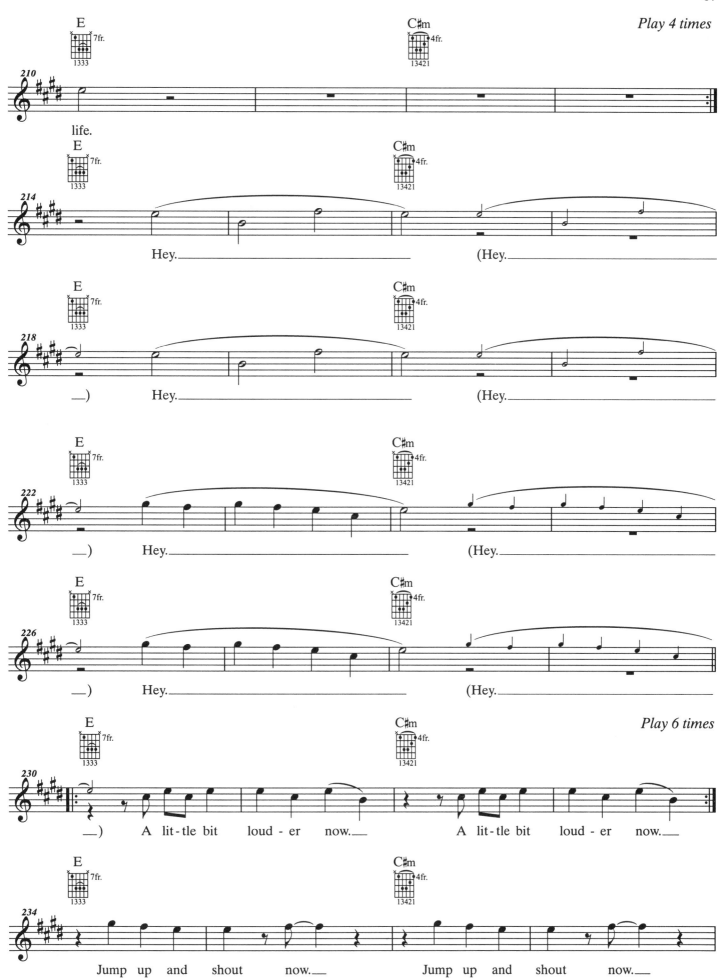

68

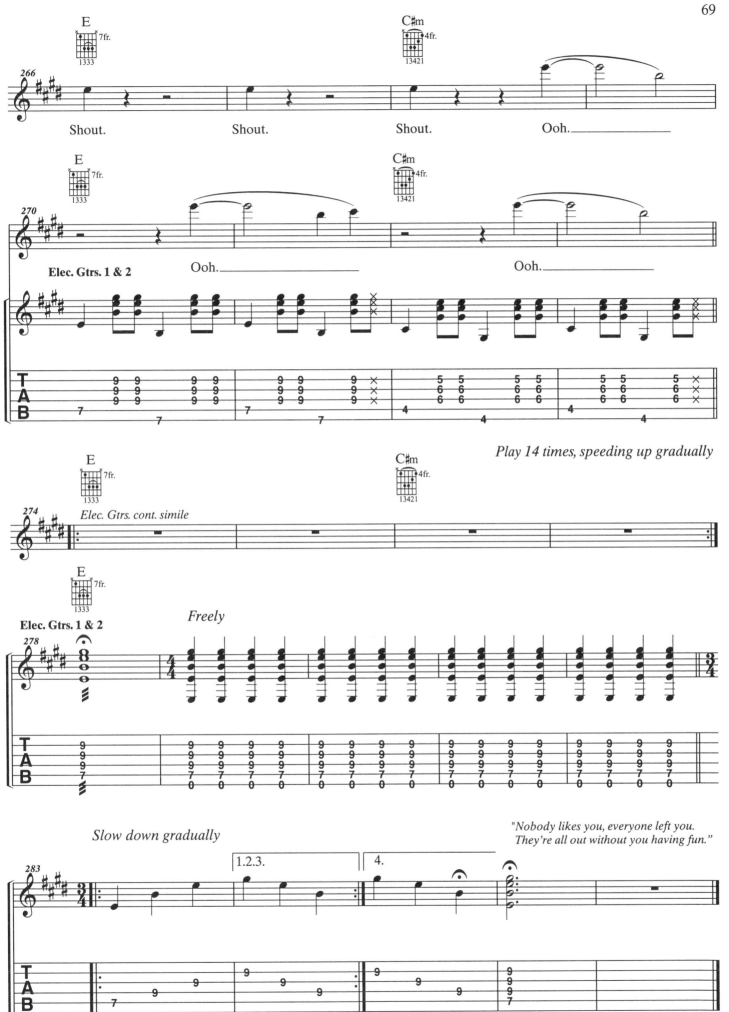

WAKE ME UP WHEN SEPTEMBER ENDS

Words by BILLIE JOE
Music by GREEN DAY

Chorus:

Here comes— the rain a-gain,—

end Rhy. Fig. 2

fall - ing from the stars.— Drenched in— my

74

75

Wake Me Up When September Ends - 9 - 6
25748

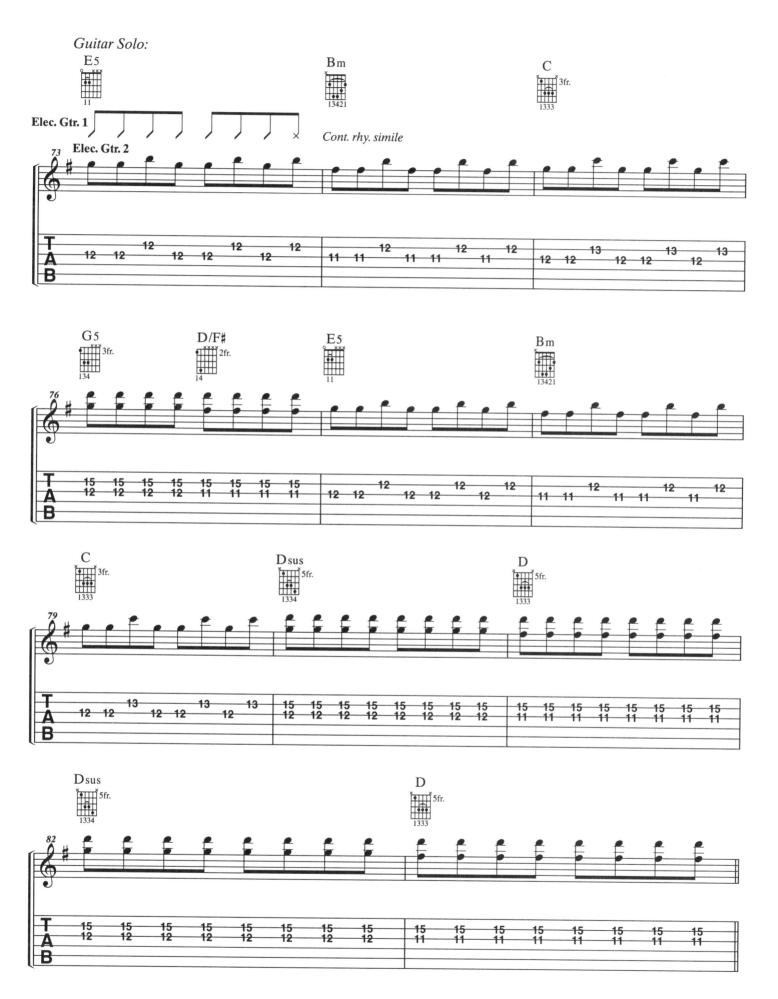

MINORITY

Lyrics by BILLIE JOE
Music by GREEN DAY

which I stand a - lone. A face in the crowd, un - sung a - gainst the mold. With -
thou - sand bro - ken hearts. "For cry - ing out loud," she screamed un - to me. A

Chorus:

Resume Chorus Fig. simile

out a doubt, sin - gled out, the on - ly way I know.
free - for - all, f*** 'em all. "You are your own sight." } 'Cause I want to be the mi -

nor - i - ty. I don't___ need your au - thor - i - ty.

Down with the mor - al ma - jor - i - ty. 'Cause___ I want to be the mi - nor - i - ty.

Bridge:

Elec.
Gtrs.
1 & 2

Cont. rhy. simile

1. Stepped out of the line_____ like a sheep runs
2. *Instrumental*

from the herd. March - ing out of time_____ to my own beat

Minority - 4 - 2
25748

82

now.   The on-ly way I know.   2. One

Interlude:

Resume Verse Fig. simile

Hey.   Hey.   Hey.   Hey.   Hey.

w/ad lib. vocal

Play 7 times

Play 3 times

N.C.
Drums
8

One

Verse 3:

All gtrs. tacet

N.C.

light,   one mind   flash-ing in the dark.   Blind-ed   by   the   si-lence   of   a

thous-sand bro-ken hearts.   "For   cry-ing out__loud,"   she screamed un-to   me.   A

BOULEVARD OF BROKEN DREAMS

Words by BILLIE JOE
Music by GREEN DAY

Moderately slow ♩ = 86

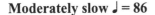

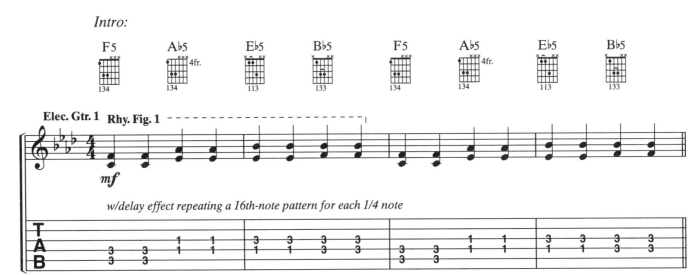

1. I walk a lone-ly road, the on-ly one that I___ have ev-er known.___
2. I'm walk-ing down the line that di-vides me___ some-where in my___

___ Don't know where it goes, but it's home to me___ and I walk a-lone.___
mind. On the bor-der-line of the edge and___ where___ I walk a-lone.___

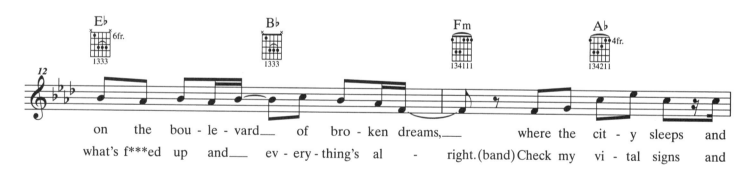

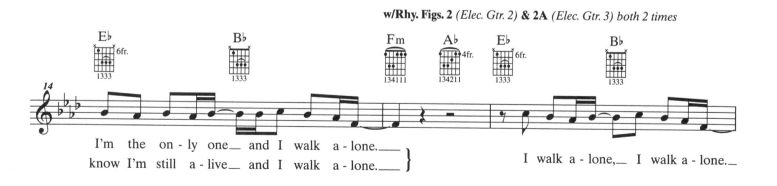

Boulevard of Broken Dreams - 6 - 4
25748

Boulevard of Broken Dreams - 6 - 6
25748

GOOD RIDDANCE (TIME OF YOUR LIFE)

Lyrics by BILLIE JOE
Music by BILLIE JOE and GREEN DAY

92

Interlude:

GUITAR TAB GLOSSARY **

TABLATURE EXPLANATION

READING TABLATURE: Tablature illustrates the six strings of the guitar. Notes and chords are indicated by the placement of fret numbers on a given string(s).

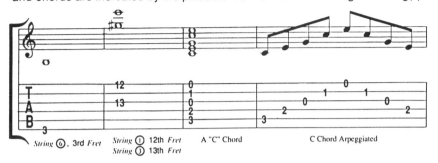

String ⑥, 3rd Fret   *String ① 12th Fret*   A "C" Chord   C Chord Arpeggiated
String ③ 13th Fret

BENDING NOTES

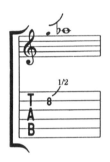

HALF STEP: Play the note and bend string one half step.*

WHOLE STEP: Play the note and bend string one whole step.

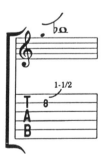

WHOLE STEP AND A HALF: Play the note and bend string a whole step and a half.

TWO STEPS: Play the note and bend string two whole steps.

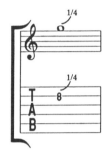

SLIGHT BEND (Microtone): Play the note and bend string slightly to the equivalent of half a fret.

PREBEND (Ghost Bend): Bend to the specified note, before the string is picked.

PREBEND AND RELEASE: Bend the string, play it, then release to the original note.

REVERSE BEND: Play the already-bent string, then immediately drop it down to the fretted note.

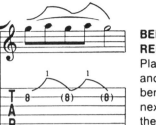

BEND AND RELEASE: Play the note and gradually bend to the next pitch, then release to the original note. Only the first note is attacked.

BENDS INVOLVING MORE THAN ONE STRING: Play the note and bend string while playing an additional note (or notes) on another string(s). Upon release, relieve pressure from additional note(s), causing original note to sound alone.

BENDS INVOLVING STATIONARY NOTES: Play notes and bend lower pitch, then hold until release begins (indicated at the point where line becomes solid).

UNISON BEND: Play both notes and immediately bend the lower note to the same pitch as the higher note.

DOUBLE NOTE BEND: Play both notes and immediately bend both strings simultaneously.

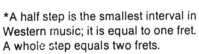

*A half step is the smallest interval in Western music; it is equal to one fret. A whole step equals two frets.

© 1990 Beam Me Up Music
c/o CPP/Belwin, Inc. Miami, Florida 33014
International Copyright Secured   Made in U.S.A.   All Rights Reserved

**By Kenn Chipkin and Aaron Stang

RHYTHM SLASHES

STRUM INDICATIONS: Strum with indicated rhythm.

The chord voicings are found on the first page of the transcription underneath the song title.

INDICATING SINGLE NOTES USING RHYTHM SLASHES: Very often single notes are incorporated into a rhythm part. The note name is indicated above the rhythm slash with a fret number and a string indication.

ARTICULATIONS

HAMMER ON: Play lower note, then "hammer on" to higher note with another finger. Only the first note is attacked.

LEFT HAND HAMMER: Hammer on the first note played on each string with the left hand.

PULL OFF: Play higher note, then "pull off" to lower note with another finger. Only the first note is attacked.

FRET-BOARD TAPPING: "Tap" onto the note indicated by + with a finger of the pick hand, then pull off to the following note held by the fret hand.

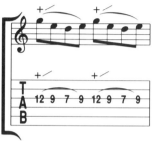

TAP SLIDE: Same as fretboard tapping, but the tapped note is slid randomly up the fretboard, then pulled off to the following note.

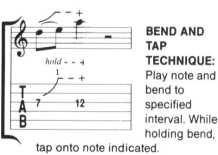

BEND AND TAP TECHNIQUE: Play note and bend to specified interval. While holding bend, tap onto note indicated.

LEGATO SLIDE: Play note and slide to the following note. (Only first note is attacked).

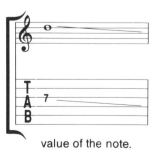

LONG GLISSANDO: Play note and slide in specified direction for the full value of the note.

SHORT GLISSANDO: Play note for its full value and slide in specified direction at the last possible moment.

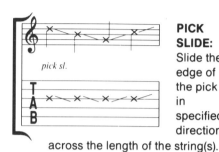

PICK SLIDE: Slide the edge of the pick in specified direction across the length of the string(s).

MUTED STRINGS: A percussive sound is made by laying the fret hand across all six strings while pick hand strikes specified area (low, mid, high strings).

PALM MUTE: The note or notes are muted by the palm of the pick hand by lightly touching the string(s) near the bridge.

TREMOLO PICKING: The note or notes are picked as fast as possible.

TRILL: Hammer on and pull off consecutively and as fast as possible between the original note and the grace note.

ACCENT: Notes or chords are to be played with added emphasis.

STACCATO (Detached Notes): Notes or chords are to be played roughly half their actual value and with separation.

DOWN STROKES AND UPSTROKES: Notes or chords are to be played with either a downstroke (⊓ ∙) or upstroke (∨) of the pick.

VIBRATO: The pitch of a note is varied by a rapid shaking of the fret hand finger, wrist, and forearm.

HARMONICS

NATURAL HARMONIC: A finger of the fret hand lightly touches the note or notes indicated in the tab and is played by the pick hand.

ARTIFICIAL HARMONIC: The first tab number is fretted, then the pick hand produces the harmonic by using a finger to lightly touch the same string at the second tab number (in parenthesis) and is then picked by another finger.

ARTIFICIAL "PINCH" HAR-MONIC: A note is fretted as indicated by the tab, then the pick hand produces the harmonic by squeezing the pick firmly while using the tip of the index finger in the pick attack. If parenthesis are found around the fretted note, it does not sound. No parenthesis means both the fretted note and A.H. are heard simultaneously.

TREMOLO BAR

SPECIFIED INTERVAL: The pitch of a note or chord is lowered to a specified interval and then may or may not return to the original pitch. The activity of the tremolo bar is graphically represented by peaks and valleys.

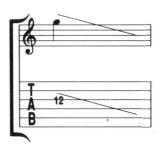

UN-SPECIFIED INTERVAL: The pitch of a note or a chord is lowered to an unspecified interval.